From Within
the Heart of God

This Book Belongs to:

Mrs. Jean Robbinson
197 Atlantic Ave
North Hampton, NH 03862

From Within the Heart of God

THE JOURNAL OF JESUS

Michael Dwinell

Copyright © 2003 by Michael Dwinell.

Library of Congress Number: 2002096954
ISBN: Hardcover 1-4010-9086-9
Softcover 1-4010-9085-0

All rights reserved. No part of this book may be reproduced or transmitted in any form or by any means, electronic or mechanical, including photocopying, recording, or by any information storage and retrieval system, without permission in writing from the copyright owner.

This book was printed in the United States of America.

To order additional copies of this book, contact:
Xlibris Corporation
1-888-795-4274
www.Xlibris.com
Orders@Xlibris.com

17634

CONTENTS

- INTRODUCTION 9
- THE DREAM 15
- WORTHY 17
- MAGDALA 19
- THE BEGINNING 21
- A VISITATION 24
- AT THE EVENING MEAL 28
- THEY DO NOT KNOW 30
- JOHN, MY FRIEND 32
- LOVER 35
- NEW WINE 38
- THEY DO NOT KNOW YOU 40
- THE MAN IN THE TREE 43
- THE DARK ONES 45
- ONLY SOME OF THEM 46
- ANOTHER DREAM 48
- TO LOVE ME 49
- MY MOTHER 51
- MY FAMILY 53
- CRIPPLED 57
- IN THEIR HANDS 61
- BLOOD 64
- ALREADY DEAD 68
- GOOD 72
- THE MOUNTAIN 74

ANOTHER DREAM 79
ANOTHER DREAM 81
MY FATHER 82
YOUR LONGING AND HEARTACHE 84
PETER, MY BROTHER 88
FOOD 90
RAGE 93
NO EXCUSES 96
KISSING 98
GENEROSITY 101
THE DREAM AGAIN 104
ABOUT THE AUTHOR 113

Dedication

TO DEBORAH ALICE
Also
I WOULD LIKE SPECIAL THANKS TO LEITH SPEIDEN FOR
THE FINAL MARY MAGDALA PIECE, AND
TO PETER BALS FOR THE PAINTING.

INTRODUCTION

I love Jesus. I have loved Jesus for a very long time, ever since I was a small boy in St. Paul's Episcopal Church's boys' and men's choir in Dedham, Massachusetts. Being in that choir meant meeting weekly for rehearsals and singing at a variety of worship services. It also meant being exposed to the 1928 Episcopal prayer book, and more importantly, being drenched in the life of a man named Jesus. The stories of Jesus in the New Testament portrayed a man like no other man I had ever known, a man steeped in integrity and courage, a man willing to speak of the hypocrisy between people's behavior and what they professed. A man who went for the deepest truth, a man who was not seducible.

Every little boy requires and seeks assistance in learning how to become a man. He needs to be taught. He needs lessons. Mostly he needs a model. I have found that model. Even though in college years I read, studied, and recognized the illumination of Mohammed and Buddha, it was Jesus who captured my heart's love, intrigued my mind, and inspired my soul. To this day He calls me into the fullness of my sacred human masculinity.

I came to know him as full—full with humanity and full

with divinity. In the fullness of his humanity, his divinity was not diminished; and in the fullness of his divinity, his humanity was not diminished. To speak of him as fully human and fully divine is to say the same thing in two different ways. This does not construct a duality, but points to a complementariness. There is no duality, only compatibility and wholeness.

To be frank, I have come to hold this Jesus in such high esteem that the modern portrayals of him in scholarship, in cinema, and in literature are not only lacking but also, often, are offensive to me. They often seem to emasculate Jesus, to make him too pious, spiritualizing him right out of his body; or they make him an "ordinary" human being who lives in a tortured, neurotic enslavement to his divinity. Or perhaps they make him an academic cipher, lost in the pages of history, behind layers of gospel editors. Sometimes he is rendered strictly an activist for social justice, or a herald for whatever cause is currently politically correct, or merely a wise teacher, or even a pathetic, passive victim. At other times he is the perfect product of a white upper-class Sunday School—neutered and polite. None of these portrayals evokes love, devotion, or inspiration. None of them has the fire necessary to burn away the dross of the ego.

With these journeys of imagination I invite the reader into an experience of Jesus as a mature, mentally healthy, robust adult in whom and through whom God has chosen to dwell in a most intimate way. Jesus himself lived within a full, direct, and intimate experience of God, the Holy One. So complete was the union between God and Jesus that Jesus had extraordinary powers and spoke of God, not as a set of religious perceptions, but rather as synonymous with the deepest structures and stratas of reality. He is fully human, fully God, and neither at the cost of the other. Yet it costs Jesus everything.

I realize that taking the step of imagining Jesus' experience at various points in his life and ministry could be considered by some to be bold, or indeed, arrogant. But imagination is the spiritual organ of the psyche. It is the soul's gift to us.

Imagination enables us to perceive and experience the ultimate reality that lies just beneath and is woven through and through penultimate reality. It enables us to receive and experience the presence of God veritably humming in and through all ordinary events. It is, therefore, arrogant and unfaithful *not* to imagine.

I do not assume that my imaginings are the only possible rendering of the experience of Jesus. These meditations come from the psychic life of the Christ within me. The inner Christ within each of us has imagination. I invite you to enter into these experiences with your own imagination to build on and deepen them and, thereby, more faithfully seek, serve, and listen to the Christ within you. Perhaps you will be inspired, be quickened to the core, and fall in love.

The following scrolls were found near the body of Mary of Magdala, who died some thirty-five years after the crucifixion of Jesus of Nazareth.

THE DREAM

Last night, the same dream again
It comes more often

I am the Rabbi, or healer of a very ancient family
So long ago, it is before the time of speech.

I stand upon the crown of a high hill.
It is also the mouth of a huge cave.
My feet rest upon the top of the cave.
In my hand is a long stick
With a gourd attached
And in the gourd there is
Honey and crushed apples.
I am reaching over and flinging
The honey and crushed apples into the cave.
There is a huge gourd of this food beside me
So there is no need to stop.
And in the cave, I know, there is a behemeth, a monster,
A terrible large wild animal.

My people believe it is my job as healer to keep the monster
    asleep
But I know
we all will perish, unless,
I rouse the monster . . .
Then each of us must enter the cave, and
Face the beast.

I will have to be the first.
I will be the first.

WORTHY

"Before I formed you in the womb,
I knew you, and
Before you were born
I consecrated you."

Fear.
The first time I heard these words,
A terrible rippling body fear.
Too young to understand.
But I knew the words as
True
True about me
So like other children in so may ways
And so not like,
In the most important way.

Mother and father loved me
More than devoted parents
Because they knew, too . . . the truth
Never spoken—only in their eyes.
Their moments of
Hesitation

Always stories—memories.
Stories and memories that spoke of my difference.
They told the story of the year Herod
Ordered all the
Boy children murdered.
They never mentioned me in the story.

But one year, in my ninth year, I knew, I knew the story was
     about me.
Since my ninth year, I have known the hugeness of my life and
Finally come to a place where I can bear it.

I wonder if I will be worthy?
But what of its outcome?
What could be so big that all those sons should die?
Was something begun in blood, be ended in blood?

Ever since I was nine
I have known that a King who never saw me
And whom I would never see
Would desire my death.

My beginning is soon to come.
That horror was about me.
About my consecration before my birth.

Every day I remember those boys in my prayers.
What is this destiny of mine
That it should be born in and paid for with
The spilling of blood.
Will I be worthy?
I anguish.

MAGDALA

Who will come with me?
Who will step in?
Who will step over?

Magdala will come.
Magdala has known me
For a very long time.

In the dust and sand as children
We were together.
We played.
We talked.
We hid.
We fought
Everywhere together.

And she knew—about me she knew, the truth.
She knew more than anyone
And she cared
And she is closest of all.

As a young man and as a young woman
We came to know each other's bodies.
She knows my body and I hers.
I know her smells, her soft skin.
The tip of her finger
And the flash of her eyes.

The body desire has been there, the blood has been hot
But we both can't
We won't even

Because she loves me
She knows it would break something in me. She renounces.
And I won't
For, indeed, something inside would break,
My real love would be betrayed.

And so she will come, step in, step over
She will watch it all, bear it all, and be there with me
Wherever it goes
However it ends.

THE BEGINNING

Steaming,
I rise up from the waters of the river,
Steaming.
Beloved John holds me tightly.
He is beaming, laughing, crying, and shouting—
Shouting my praises, shouting my bigness, shouting my power,
Shouting his love for me;
And I am full, filled with fullness.

All about me
Things are in motion,
But nothing moves.
There are lots of noises,
But all is utterly quiet and still.
Everything stops still—
Utterly still.
The sun is bright.
The air—radiant.
I've never seen so clearly in my life.

I am full. Everything is full.
Him
Them
It all becomes us
One.
Utter stillness.
It lasts forever and but an instant,

And then suddenly,
I see dear John's face,
His teeth, his eyes, his hair
And I feel the water moving over my body.

In the next moment,
In the blink of an eye,
I am alone deep in the wilderness,
Alone with my fullness and my bigness.
All the years of waiting,
All the years of preparation,
All the prayer and study,
Blessed and fulfilled beyond measure,
Fuller, fuller, fuller
And bigger and bigger than I could ever imagine.
I am filled with huge splendor,
Enormous beauty, shining brilliance, fullness of spirit,
And immense new knowledge.
I am light-headed, mirthful.
I can rise above the horrors
Above the suffering
Above the death.
I think I can fly!
Fly!
Lift up and fly!

How to hold these blessings?
How to live with this magnificence?
How to contain all this energy?
How to focus?

I must not fly.
I must not make this *mine*.
This must not be about *me*.
No tricks, no spectacles, no magic.
I want to fly. I can feel the air.
I can imagine the soaring
I want to fly!
To play with this bigness, this fullness—

To change one stone to a loaf of bread—
Just one!
To step off of a high place and fly just once,
Just once.
It must not be mine.
I must not let this become mine.

Such a temptation to fly,
To prance through life
As the magical, beloved trickster.
And the knowing,
The certain knowing deep in the bones
That I absolutely must not.
I cannot.

I will not violate my true love.
I will not let my heart be exploited.

A VISITATION

Long cold nights,
Moon and rain,
And still, the desire to fly
To rise above,
To leave the earth,
To spring away, to float off.

Exhausted, I lay there,
Exhausted, exhausted,
Famished, thirsty, parched, filthy dirty.
I lay on my back,
And I face the rising sun,
Alone, alone.

Immediately,
There is another pair of eyes.
Eyes looking down upon me.
Not eyes of a brother or sister.
The eyes of a cat,
A large mountain cat. She had waited until I was exhausted.
She stalks me and waits,

Patiently, and carefully,
And now she has me.
I am her food, her reward for that patience.
I am a meal.
Is she the monster of the dream?

There will be no flying,
For I am about to die.
No escape.
No rising above or floating off.
Her eyes watch me
And their piercing sight rivets me to the earth.

I am animal.
I am prey.

I am the food for her life
Milk for her cubs.
I am about to die,
And I am rooted to that place,
In that place, to my body,
In that body;
And I am mortal and ordinary,
And no better or worse than she,
No more or less necessary to creation.

I wonder
If it is all going to come to this end—
All the preparation, all the praying, all the waiting,
All the excitement, to come to this natural end.

And I know terror,
Stark terror,
Far surpassing fear, terror to the balls of my feet,
Terror so my bowels let loose,
And no sound comes out of my mouth.

And then
Without a sound
Or second thought,
She simply leaves,
Turns and leaves.
Beyond belief!
Beyond belief!
And I will never understand why.

Breathing comes back.
I can move.
My heart slows
And I cough,
A sound comes out,
And relief—
Incredible relief.
I sit up
And weep
And weep
And weep
For joy!
Tears of cleansing
For joy! To be alive!
To be alive with her,
With the earth
In my body, to feel life. Never have I felt so much joy!
Full with joy!

No longer
Thoughts of floating off,
Of rising up to fly,
Of leaving,
Of making the bigness mine.

I am here, ... here ...
Full of God,
Full.
I am here utterly full of beauty
Inside and out,
With God.
And glad,
Glad beyond words

Grateful
To be here.

There is no better place,
There is no better place
To which one might fly.
Utterly glad

To be here with this body,
Overflowing with God
One with all.

AT THE EVENING MEAL

The evening air brought her presence to me first.
Such rich and provocative smells, her perfume.
Beautiful in bright colors and subtle folds.
And radiant oiled black hair almost long enough to touch the
   floor.

How did she know?
Was she sent?
And how did she dare?
She came directly to me
Eyes never leaving mine
She knew.
Behind me she stood.
I seated and she standing with her hands on my shoulders
She touched me.
Because she knew and dared and touched, she wept.
She wept out all her tears
A lifetime of tears

My face was wet. My neck was wet. My head was wet. My feet were wet.
And then she gathered up that gorgeous hair to wash me and to dry me.
With such tenderness and delicacy that the tears also came to my eyes,
How did she know?
Her willingness to come into a place where she was not allowed and not wanted.
Her willingness to risk it all—herself, her heart.
The intensity of her love for me—with no reservations—
Made her whole.
No flower, not even one in paradise, was more beautiful than her in that moment.
Such beauty erupting in a wasteland of righteousness and piety and barren sanctity.
It was all I could do to sit still
And allow her to give to me, to allow myself to receive her.
I was filled up and spilled over.
My heart broke wide open.

She gave to me
What I give others
I could hardly bear it.
I understand why it is hard for them.

THEY DO NOT KNOW

Followers everywhere
The numbers grow
There is joy in them and gladness.
From the Word there is joy and hope.
They are coming to know the joy and freedom
Of the Kingdom At Hand.

Like little children.
For they do not know,
How could they know
The rest of it.

I tell them
And soon enough they will see.
They will see it in my own life soon enough.
To go down this road
This road to Jerusalem,
This road to You.
Is to be caught up in something huge
Gathered up in something beautiful.
It is all there is

And it gives everything and asks for everything.
To go down this road is to fall in love.
The fire is so hot, the love is so deep
All other loves
All other loyalties
Are burnt away
Everything else becomes second
You are everything and the love of You is everything.
I try to tell them if they go down this road
That they must.
They do not know.

JOHN, MY FRIEND

For twelve days
No words.
Twelve days and nights in a lonely place,
Silence,
Alone,
With my devastation.

Beheaded.
Told me he was beheaded
Simply to feed the blood lust of a young daughter.
To satiate the fantasy of an old man.
They passed his head around
On a serving dish
As if it were the head of a wild beast,
Hunted,
Hunted for food,
For sport.

He was ferocious.
My cousin.
My closest friend.
Cradling me at my baptism.
Both of us raised by the same holy milk.
Both of us compelled as truth speakers
And seekers of the author of truth,
As lovers of the author of truth.
The same milk, both of us.

I'm so heavy with grief and horror.
John slaughtered.
On my account.
It cleaves me like a sword
From crown to pit

And ripped open and all the old wounds,
I feel them all,
The little babies and now John,
I suspect there will be many more.
I am splayed wide open!
No protection.
No hiding.
This grief is so exhausting,
And yet it will not let me sleep.
This grief is so full of pain and rage;
And yet I feel more tender and more soft.

At first, I hated them, detested them
They who did this to John.
They who made a mockery of him.
They who toyed with his life
And his death.

I hated them.
And the hate felt good.
I thought perhaps that I would hate them
For the rest of my life.

And I
Discovered in hating them
I had taken them in—
Way in.
In my openness,
In my ripped-wide openness,
And in my hatred,
They had come way in.
And I began instead to hold them.
And I found
They had room in my heart
For whoever they are
And the horrors of their lives . . . room.

John was first out into the desert.
First as proclaimer and provoker.
And yet again, he led the way.
He taught me.
He taught me how to love the tormentors.

This thing called "grief" makes an opening
For the fire of Holy Love.

LOVER

Grandfather Job, wise one,
You are in my heart,
And before my eyes.
I sleep at night
And wake to find
You still there.
I see you standing,
Ravished by your travails,
Almost crushed
Under the outrageousness
Of your unjust suffering.
Body and soul sorely wounded,
And yet still standing,
Standing before Him.
Face to face with Him.
Never has any man
Had so much justice on his side.
Never was any man
So entitled
To complaint and compensation.
Never was any man

So privileged to rage
Into His face
And demand redress and requital,
Never;
And yet,
This is what I see.

He spoke but once,
You saw His face,
You felt His breath,
And you fell,
Fell to your knees,
Weeping,
In great sorrow.
You apologized.
You wept,
Said, "I am sorry,"
And repented.
You loved Him.
You loved Him.
You were driven
To your knees by love.

In an instant,
In a blink,
Your rage
And your righteousness
Were gone.
Your just cause was surrendered,
Forgotten,
No complaint nor sorrow nor regret.

What is it?
What is it
About hearing His voice,
And seeing His face

And feeling His breath,
that instantly
Makes a man His lover,
His passionate lover?
And everything else
No longer matters.
I am coming to know
Of this myself.

NEW WINE

Of course the beginning
Was a marriage.
It could be no other way.
The bonding
Of improbable and impossible
Contradictions summoning up
A never before seen,
Utterly new creation.
The Kingdom
And the creation present
In the same time and in the same space,
Male and female,
Spirit and flesh,
Good and evil,
Life and death,
Human and God—
Paradox
The great wedding, the great Holy Marriage
Into which we are all plunged.

Right from the start
They missed.
They knew I had special "gifts."
So, when they ran out of wine,
In their need,
They came to me.
They thought that my powers
Were about helping things to
Go along comfortably
As they always had.
No change, nothing new.

But I could only make
For them a new wine—only
A wine they had never tasted before,
A wine awakening and shocking the tongue,
A wine so new that it could
Not be contained in any
Of the old containers.
Even Mary did not understand.

The drinking of this wine,
Will be so very new,
For this wine,
When swallowed
And digested
Turns to blood, the very blood of life itself.

Here,
At the great holy marriage.
This joyous beginning
Is the foretaste of the end.
Old wine, new wine, blood.
It's always present.
Never far off.

THEY DO NOT KNOW YOU

They strut
Like finely-feathered birds,
Publicly preening,
Hung in finery.
They chant memorized prayers.
They live by formulas of purity.
They mark each other
By race and birth.
They count themselves as righteous and superior.

Sad,
They think it all matters to You.
That You are impressed.
That You will shower them
With some wonderful favor
For their specialness.

Saddest of all,
Their strutting and their displays
And their public self-acclamation
Reveal that they do not know You,
Not at all.
They know their
Self-serving idea of You,
But You, they do not know.

For You are the one
In whom there is everything
In whom there is Paradise and Sheol.
You are the one
Who makes the rain fall on the just
And the unjust.
In You there is creation and destruction.
In You there is great joy and great sorrow.

In You there is light and darkness.
In You there is the birth of the newborn and the slaughter of the newborn.
In You there is peace and horror.

You do not know Yourself
As special,
Or pretty,
Or pure,
Or superior.
You are the one with
The broken heart and a contrite spirit.
You, Holy One,
Are broken-hearted
And humbled by Your own being,
Overwhelmed by
Your own suffering of Your allness,
Confronted by Your own apprehension of Yourself.

And I love You for your courage,
Your willingness to bear Yourself.
And I love You for Your splendor and Your fullness.

So,
So You seek the lost and wounded and empty
For Your companions.
Those who come to You with no superiority,
No illusion of purity,
No claim whatsoever to be justified.
They know You,
And You know them.
For they are telling their truth
Which is Your truth,
And they are living Your truth,
Which is their truth.

We will bear
In our bodies
Your broken-heartedness,
And Your contriteness;
And thus we will be Your Companions.
And You will be our Lover.

You need many of us,
Many,
Many to be Companions—
Companions to You.

THE MAN IN THE TREE

The man in the sycamore tree
On the streets of Jericho,
His unknown hunger
And desire for You
Urged him to climb the tree.
He was too short
To see me,
Yet he knew he must see me.
This man, empty, corrupt—collector of taxes.

The evening meal
With him
At his home
Was generous, and it was awkward.
He was a gracious householder,
And he did not know what to do with himself.

He thought that seeing me was enough,
But I saw him,
And I called him by name,
And I made him my host for dinner.

He found himself sitting
In what had been his even unknown
And deeper hidden desire.
He had been seen,
Named, called out
And made a host,
A host of his own beloved,

And much to his surprise,
Knew that that is what he wanted all along.
And that You wanted him.
It will take him
A long time to answer to his new name
"Companion."

THE DARK ONES

It's always
The dark ones
Who know me first.

In the name of
Protection and safety
They crush out
Hope and desire.
They know the truth—
If my words are heard
If my breath is breathed in
They will be silenced and dethroned.

ONLY SOME OF THEM

They like, . . . No,
They love being with me.
They like this new adventure.
They like who they are
And who they are becoming
While in my presence,
And I delight in them also.
These twelve,
They are good to be with.
And watching them
In spite of their complaints
Come alive and blossom
And bear fruits is such a pleasure.
They are
More often than not
A blessing to have with me on this journey.

It will be hard for them;
Very hard,
Indeed, when I am gone.
Hard because their becoming,
Their blossoming,
Their fruitfulness
Was not visible in them
Before me.
With my departure,
It may all vanish.
It will be very hard.

And only some of them
Will come to hold
Their fruitfulness
As their own.

For only some will it
Continue to grow and spread,
And they will take the passion
On very long journeys,
Into lands I never have been to.
And they will come to understand
That this becomes possible,
Not in spite of my going,
But precisely because of it.

They will come to know
That in looking at me
They were seeing themselves.

But, for now,
They love being with me,
And I, them.
And that is very good.

ANOTHER DREAM

I am to plant a tree,
A young sapling;
There are others
Whom I don't know,
Who have a clear sense of where
The tree should be planted.
In fact, they have already dug a large hole
In the earth for the root ball of my tree.
It is a hole
Within a grove of other trees,
In which they or their forbearers have,
Likewise, planted;
And I know
That my tree
Must not go into that hole, not that hole.
I must dig and dig
And find another place
Elsewhere.

TO LOVE ME

Today,
I asked them
If they loved me.
There was no response.
They were mute.
They could not answer.
I want them to love me.
Often, people do not love me.
They admire.
They respect.
They adore.
They worship.
But they make me
Too much different from them
To really love me.
I see things they do not see.
Magdala loves me.

I want them to love me,
And they need
To learn to love me.
The whole thing
Will fall apart, I will fail
If they do not learn
To love me.
They will never
Truly love themselves,
Until they learn
To love me.
They will always
Think that I alone
Am the carrier

Of this Word, this breath,
Unless they learn to love me.
They will always know
Themselves
As inadequate children,
Unless and until they learn to love me.

So, of course, I will ask them
Again and again,
"Do you love me?"
Unless they find their souls,
Unless they find in themselves
Enough to love me,
They will never
Be able to know
Your love for them,
Nor to know
The depth of the desire
You have for them to love You.

MY MOTHER

Only once did she speak of it,
The terrifying night when The Presence visited her.
She had just barely come into her first blood,
Still a girl.
In the darkest of the night,
Her room was filled with a huge presence—
Some huge, male voice that commanded her,
That demanded her,
That spoke of God and sex and birth.
She had never before
Seen maleness naked,
And here he was
Many times larger than human.
She said she had never been so afraid.
There was no way to understand.
First her body said yes
Then her heart
And finally her mouth said yes.
Beyond her fear
She said yes, yes,
One hundred times yes.

And just as suddenly,
The messenger left.
The room was dark,
Only the pungent odor remained
No sleep that night.

My mother has suffered much,
And will suffer much more.

MY FAMILY

Sleep will not come tonight.
My bowels feel they
Are holding thick,
Wet mud,
And there is a stone in my chest
Where my heart should be.

Today was hard,
Very difficult.
I was speaking and teaching,
And I was surprised by the presence
Of my mother and my brothers.
They had come to take me away.
Concerned for my well-being.
They were afraid
A demon
Had taken over my tongue.
Mostly, they were embarrassed for themselves,
For the family,
Because everybody
In the village knew them

And knew me.
They told me I had to come away
Because of my wild talk about God.
Whether I spoke truth or not,
It would hurt the family.
It would bring shame to the family.
They told me I was being disloyal
And that God
Would not want me
To be disloyal to the family.
And they said this
In front of everyone
So that everyone could hear.
I think they said it
Expecting fully
That I would be silent,
And I would go with them.

And so,
I knew I must be utterly clear,
And I spoke clarity
Knowing I would hurt my brothers,
I would hurt
And humiliate my mother,
I would bring more pain

To her life.
She already has suffered
So much pain and shame and suffering
Because of my birth.

Yet, I had to speak,
And speak hard,
Hard words;
Words that would twist old wounds
In her
Wounds opened again and rip them deeper.

Everyone must understand
That family,
Blood family,
Is not the Kingdom of heaven,
And that loyalty to family
Is not faithfulness;
And that belonging to family
Is not salvation.

Oh, Holy One,
You give so very much
And You ask for as much
As You give.
It is hard, very hard.

And so I spoke to my mother.
I stunned her
And stung her.
I stunned her
With my words.
She was rocked and stunned.
I banished her from my presence.
I told her to get away,
To leave me alone,
To go home,
And to take my brothers with her.
I told her
That she was not my mother.
They were not my family,
And they had
No claim on me whatsoever.
I told her that the
Only real connection between people
Was between people who chose

To live in and out
Of the desire of God,
And she was silenced
And the tears flooded down her face.
And she stood there for
A long time in silence,
And I said not any more words.
And finally she turned
And left
And walked away,
And everyone else was in mute silence.
The words had to be spoken.
What a cost.
This night, I cannot sleep.
The ground is too hard.
My bowels are turmoil.
How many more times will I have to speak
Like this?

CRIPPLED

These rough hands of mine,
Large and strong,
Wounded and scarred
Years of working
With the wood and the tools,
Able and practiced.
And this hand
With the long scar across
To the thumb
When I was careless
With the hammer.

And now
They are put to a new use.
With spittle and dirt,
I place my hands
On the eyes
Of those who have never seen,
And they see.
The skin of my hand
Touches the skin

Of a cripple's leg,
And he walks.
I lay my hands upon another,
And from deep
Within my bowels,
With full attention
And entering into his woundedness,
Something gathers within me
And moves
And we three enter into wholeness—
The cripple,
Me,
The Holy One.

And so now, they look upon these hands
And they see
The hands of a healer.
They see hands that heal,
And they call upon me
To make them well.
And they do not understand
That The Wholeness
Is by You
And for You,
And includes us all.
I touch them,
Oh Beloved,
Because in their crippledness
And woundedness,
I know places
That are crippled and wounded
In me;
And I know Your
Crippledness and woundedness.

Just today,
One
Who should never have
Spoken to me,
A Synophonecian and a woman,
Boldly and courageously
Demanded that I heal her daughter.
How did she know
I was a healer?
It must have been
The love of her daughter
That overcame the terrible risk

She took even speaking to me.
So I spoke back
To her
What I thought to be
The truth—
That I was only
To involve myself
With the children of Israel,
The Hebrew household.
And she, with all the rage
In her thin, frail body,
Screamed at me,
"Even the dogs are allowed
To lick the crumbs
Up from under the table."

I was stunned!
No one
Had ever screamed at me like that
So foully cursed me
I could smell her rage.
Her passion was immense.

I wonder
If I could ever display
My passion that openly.
But even more,
I was stunned
By the utter truth
Of what she had said.
And she revealed to me my ignorance.

The moment the words
Entered my ears,
I knew she was right!

I was wrong
I stood in need of her forgiveness.
Of course, of course, of course!
There is nothing that is
That is not Your household.
Nothing. Absolutely nothing.
I had thought I knew You,
Oh Holy One,
All of You,
You in your entirety.
I was wrong.

And so her daughter
Was made whole,
But so was I.
Were You changed, too?
It's always that way—both.
Perhaps, she was an angel.

These rough and scarred
Hands are for everyone.
They hold everything.

IN THEIR HANDS

Again,
Today, I tried to teach them—
The twelve.
I stood in the middle
Of a large gathering
Circled about me,
Speaking and teaching,
Well beyond the sun's mid-heaven.
They were hungry
And thirsty—
Of course they would be!

And I said to the twelve,
"Gather up whatever food there might be,"
And they brought
To me
A few small fish
And fragments of bread.

Very long faces
And sorrowful eyes,
"There is not enough, not nearly enough,"
They said.
"Not even the beginnings of enough
To feed all of these.
Not even enough to feed ourselves."

I made them
Put out their hands,
And into each pair
Of hands
I placed a portion

Of bread,
And a portion of fish,
And instructed them to
Go feed the multitude.

They looked at me
As if I
Was one possessed.

I instructed them again,
"Go feed the multitude."
And so
With their tiny,
Not enough,
Portions
Cupped in their hands,
They left the center,
And went to the edge,
And fed the multitude.

And when they
Were finished,
There were great amounts
Left over.

Some said,
I had performed a miracle,
But the miracle
Took place
In the hands of the twelve
When

When they
Left the center
And went to the edge.

Perhaps now,
They will understand
That we all always live
In two worlds
At the same time,
And in the same place.
In one world,
There is never enough;
And in the other world there
Is grace and glory
And more than enough.
Two worlds—
The
Center, and the edge.
And the movement between.

Oh, yes, the kingdom
Of God is at hand,
Indeed.

BLOOD

The energy went all out of me.
I was drained empty.
And then just as suddenly,
I was filled all up
With someone else's passion,
Ardor, desire.
I turned to see
And saw blood,
Everywhere blood.
She was covered
With her own blood,
Her dress,
Her legs;
And she had crawled
Through the crowd
On her hands and knees,
And had left a trail
Of her own blood.
My vision was spinning.
The blood of the children,
The blood of John,

My blood,
My wine,
The wetness of life,
And the wetness of death,
Blood everywhere.
By all that is holy,
She should not have touched me.
A woman unclean
And doubly unclean
By the great flow

Of her birthing blood
Should not have touched me.
And all about me were mute.

But again,
Here is yet another
Who has put her eyes upon me
And dared to see.
She saw and she knew,
And she knew and she dared.
She dared to risk.
Everything
Could have been taken from her.
Because she knew
Her whole heart,
No holding back.
Whatever it is in me
That rises up in me,
That wells up, and pours forth,
That place that rises up
From within my heart
And pours forth,
It leaps out
To meet her
When she touches me.

And she was made whole.
Her blood made her whole.
I did not decide
To make her whole.
You,
Who are the bigger
Than I am
And live in me,
Moved
And made her whole.
And as always,
Something in me was enlarged,
Made whole,
Made ready
For what is coming.

And I know what's coming
For I saw them standing not far off.
Like a clump of weeds,
The pompous ones,
The hypocrites in robes,
Whispering,
Pointing,
Deciding what they must
Do about me.
All their rules
Are shattered by me,
And I don't even know
that I'm doing it.
I can see the blood
Already on their hands.
Blood will come.
Yet I stood her up,

And she bled no more.
Took her into my arms,
Embraced her,
And this night,

Some of her blood
Is on my robe and upon my hands.
And some night,
Perhaps,
She may drink my blood.
My blood will grant your desire.

ALREADY DEAD

I will arrive tomorrow,
And already
He will be dead.
Dead a long time,
And they will show
Their displeasure.
They will rail at me,
And they will want
To know
Why I took so long.
They will be enraged
At my delay,
Because in their minds,
If I had not delayed,
Lazarus would not have died.
And I will go
To where he is entombed
And wrapped,
And call him out.

And he will be alive
Again
In this world,
And they will be amazed.

But I am here tonight
With myself,
Grinding my teeth,
And wanting to throw rocks,
Heavy ones.
Will they never understand?
Who do they think I am?

And what
Do they think I am about?
And who
Do they think You are?

Two days ago
They came to me breathless,
Telling me that Lazarus
Was very ill,
And that I must
Make haste,
Because if I came quickly,
I could save his life.
So, I chose to delay
And take the long way.

They understand so little,
And from time to time,
My patience runs thin.

They do not understand
That everything
That is,
Was,
And shall be,
Is already within You,
That alive,
Or dead,
We are in You.
Alive or dead,
We are Yours.

And that when we die,
We leave here,
But there is nowhere else to go,
Because we have been already
Within You.
So calling him out
Of the tomb will be easy.
I dearly wish they understood.

And worse still,
They think,
Even my dearest ones think,
That I am here for them,
Somehow to make their lives
Go less painfully,
More smoothly,
To rescue them from wounds
And death.

I wonder
If they will ever understand
That I am here for You.
That we are all here

For You,
For Your desire,
To be in the dominion of Your heart.
So,
I chose to let him die,
And I will call him out;
And even then,
I doubt they will understand.

GOOD

Good
He tried to call me, "good."
He wanted me to be "good."
Good, clean, pure, innocent.
So being close to me
Would mean
That he too
Could be good,
Clean, and innocent.

Not true, not true, not true.
All those yearnings
To wear
The mantle of goodness
And innocence,
Must be put away.
For there is no truth in them.

And worse yet,
They invite me to forget
Who and what I really am.
And even worse,
They come between You and me.

Do not call me
"Good."

THE MOUNTAIN

Some people thought me harsh
The way I spoke to Peter.
My words were strong.
I wanted so much for Peter to see
The urgency of what had just happened.
I wanted them, the twelve,
To know, especially Peter,
That everything had changed
A new direction,
A new goal,
The end of teaching,
Preaching and healing.
And now, a new necessity
To go to Jerusalem, to end this,
To make sacrifice.

I had climbed the mountain
To be by myself,
To pray,
To renew,
As I had gone aside many times before.

I wanted quiet.
I wanted to be in Your presence,
To hear Your still,
Quiet voice.

But this time, this time,
It was different,
Entirely different,
Frighteningly different.
He came close.
Closer than He has ever been.

So close that if You had a face,
It would be too close to see.
I was inside Your heart.
Inside.
I was within the heart
Of the You,
Within the heart
A huge cavernous place, all around
Filled with throbbing pulse
And beat
And filled even more
With longing,
Desire,
Yearning,
Love.
This was the beast of my dream,
And I was in the heart of the beast;
And the heart of the beast is desire.

Desire for me.
Desire for all of us.
Desire to be one with us
And with you.
Desire not to be separated or alienated.

Anguished,
Anguished desire to be forgiven
For Your own monstrous darkness.
Desire to be loved and to love.
To know and be known,
To be one.
Your heart is so full
Of unrequited and unfinished love.

The terrible wound
Of such an unspeakably huge desire to love
And be loved.
Or, not being able
Without our help,
Without our help.
Without our help.

I thought I had known love before,
Both the giving and the receiving
Mary and John
My mother and my father,
And my love for You.
But the sweet terrible poignancy of You wounded
And anguished desire
Filled every space in my body,
And changed all of me forever.
So that now that is all there is.
Everything else becomes as smoke.
No longer is it enough
To witness to Your kingdom,
To teach about You,
To prophesy through Your truths
To heal in Your name,
No longer enough.
No,
There is only a "Yes."

"Yes, yes, again I say yes, I will.
I will give You what you need
And what You want."
It is my complete and total desire to meet Your desire,
And I will.
The space in my heart is now so huge.

And the urgency,
Is not just the power
And pitch of Your desire,
It is also
That You need not just me
To say yes,
You need many,
Many,
Many more to come to know You,
To fall in love with You,
To desire,
To say "yes" to Your desire.

And how will I say "yes?"
How will I give You what You want?
How will I help You love and be loved,
To become one with us.

I know the way.
I know the truth of it.
I learned it from the beheading of John.
I will die
And Your heart will open wider
And know deeper,
Fuller love.
I know the way.
I know the truth,
And I know that in my dying,

You will live, live more, love more, there will be more of You in
    the world
And that—just that
Is my deepest desire.
The Son of Man must go to Jerusalem
And be crucified.

ANOTHER DREAM

Last night,
I dreamt that I was carried up
To the very top
Of a steep mountain
On the back of a small mule.
The beast was so strong
And so sure-footed,
Never missed a step.
Some of the way up
Seemed impossible,
Yet the mule knew.

Now we were at the top,
The very top,
And it is time to go down,
And the way down
Is every bit as steep
As the way up.
It looks as if it was almost
Straight down.
I cannot imagine going beyond that edge

To go
Down without pitching over
The top of the mule
And dying.
I cannot imagine the mule
Being able to carry me
Down sure-footedly.
This is truly impossible,

But on the back of the mule
I must descend.
I must trust this beast.
The one who carried me to the top,
I must trust him even more.

ANOTHER DREAM

Someone is kneeling
At the bottom of a cross,
A cross mounted in the ground
Used for crucifixion.
There is somebody nailed
To that cross
Whose face I do not see.
The kneeler is weeping
And kissing HIS feet
And telling him how much he loves him.

MY FATHER

As the darkness gathers
This evening,
I hear my own voice
Saying the words,
"The son of man must go to Jerusalem and be crucified."
I hear myself
Saying those words
Again and again.
I hardly believe I am saying them,
But they are mine,
And I will say them again,
For this is what I choose,
And I will have to re-choose
It every day and
Every night until it's done.

The face of Joseph,
My dear, dear father,
Comes before me.
Sometimes I miss him
In a terribly painful way.

I wish I might have shared
My manhood with him.
These times especially.
Before he died,
He taught me
With such great patience,
All that he knew
About wood and the fashioning of wood.
And how to shape
And craft the pieces
In such a way
That they fit together

Perfectly and seamlessly.
On a day
Shortly before his death,
He handed me a gift
He had made.
It is beautiful,
Polished light and dark woods,
Grained and oiled,
Perfectly joined—
A cross,
Larger than I could hold
In the palm of my hand,
That he gave me with tears in his eyes.
I now understand his tears,
And I cry myself to sleep.
Dear, dear Joseph.

YOUR LONGING AND HEARTACHE

Like a swollen river in Spring,
This great sadness
Rises up within me
Like a baby in a mother's belly—
Ever-deepening,
Ever-increasing sadness.
I look about,
And I see.
I see.
I see.
I see the brokenness,
The woundedness,
The suffering, the fear,
The pain, the degradation,
The lostness
Of every single human being.
And I know that every human
Living or dead,

Or yet to be,
Will in like manner,
Suffer.

Oh Jerusalem,
Jerusalem, I weep for you—
And all the cities.

And You, oh Holy One,
I see You, too.
I see their suffering
As reflecting Your suffering

Of Your thwarted longing,
I see the stunning beauty of Your helplessness,
Of Your unfulfilled desire.

The whole universe rings,
Rings with the ache
Of Your heart.
And this seeing of them,
This seeing of You,
Is all I see,
And is everything I see.
There is nothing
Else to see.

And with my whole being
I desire,
I desire,
I love. I want
To do.
To give.
To move.
To share.
And soon,

Soon this sadness
Will burst open.
The streams will burst their banks.
The water will break
And the baby will come.
Breaking out to life.
Soon this sadness

Will break out
And pour forth.

I know
That I am the seed,
The seed that must
Fall to the ground

And break open and rot.
I am.
I am the seed.
My life and my death
Will end this impass,
Will bring it to a close.
Not repair it.
Not fix it.
End it.
Something new,
Something unexpected,
Unpredictable,
Will rise up,
And I,
This life of mine,
This body of mine,
Is the very seed, the very food.

Your desire will be met.
Your longing will be fulfilled.
The ache of Your heart
Will become as joy.

And they will become
One with You,
And You with them,
And their lives
Will be
Lived
Inside of You,
Not separate from You;
And their suffering
Will be bathed
In the blood of Your heart.

No longer victims
Of their own birth—
Now ardent lovers of You.
And I am the seed.
The seed
That will both
Bring the old
To an end,
And this new thing to a beginning.
The sadness is swelling
To its ripening.

PETER, MY BROTHER

Last night,
It rose up
Like a huge wave
From within my lower self,
And tears ran down my face.
Joy,
Finally joy.
      They were out
On the lake
In a small boat
Dark, windy, dangerous water,
Rowing with all their strength,
And I came to them.
At first,
They were terrified.
I could see
On their faces
They thought me a demon.
      Then Peter, yes Peter,
He dared; he tried;
He risked it all.

He stepped out of the boat
And walked two,
Three steps towards me.
He risked everything.
He dared.
Finally,
Finally, someone dared
To come across;

And for a moment,
My loneliness was broken.

When he stumbled
And started to fall,
I caught him in my arms
And held him tightly
To my chest.
We both wept.
"Peter, Peter, my brother, Peter."
He dared.
He tried.
He risked.
He came over.
And I was filled with joy.

FOOD

I have told them
That men must be fished,
Netted,
Dragged on board,
And brought ashore . . .
For You.
I have told them
That the wheat
Must be cut down,
Harvested,
Bundled, threshed,
And the chaff burnt away . . .
For You.
I have told them
That they are lamp oil
To be burnt for light,
Salt to be dispensed
To preserve and flavor meat.

I have told them
I am the vine,
You are the vine dresser,
And they are to be branches
Bearing fruit for You.
I have told them
I am the shepherd,
And they are the sheep,
Fleece and food for You.

And now I tell them
That the Son of Man
Must, needs to Jerusalem go,

And there be crucified . . .
For You.
I will stand
Before them at the meal
And hold up the bread,
And tell them it is my body,
Offered and broken . . .
For You.
And I will show them the wine,
And tell them it is my blood,
Spilt . . .
For You.

I will tell them
To do likewise . . .
For You.
And I wonder
If they will understand,
Understand
That their deepest needs,
The hunger of their hearts

Is only met
When they can become food . . .
For You.
When they meet Your deepest need . . .
To eat and digest
What You have created,
Fished,
Harvested.

Bodies,
Hearts and souls.
I wonder.

RAGE

Today I was savage.
I remember
The tiny woman who upbraded me
And the passion of her rage.
The one who told me
That even the dogs
Get to lick up the crumbs.
And I remember wondering
If I would ever dare
To let myself escape
My passion that way,
And today I did.
I was savage.

What I saw at the temple,
I could not believe.
I stood and watched,
And watched for a long time,
For a very long time;
And I could not find
One thing

That was true or right.
It was sham
And corruption
And falsehood.
I wanted to find
One thing
That was right—
Just one,
And I think I would
Have restrained myself.
I could find nothing.

And I heard her scream
For justice
And truth
In my ears,
And felt it in my body.
And with a whip in my hand,
I savaged the place.
I overturned tables.
I smashed open
The doors of animal
And bird cages. I threw money
Into the crowd,
And I whipped men.

I saw their blood.
And the memory
Of John's eyes,
And the touch of his kiss,
And of his severed head
Was with me.
And I raged,
And there was none
Who could stop me.

I am emptied, cleansed, purified,
Yes, purified for what is to come.
Purified—purged
And made ready
For what is to come.
Burned clean.

Oh, Holy One,
Your breath is so hot.
It both melts me,
And I am hardened.

NO EXCUSES

Tree, tree, Oh, tree,
Growing thing.

My time has come.
I am
On the way
To Jerusalem.
The kingdom of Heaven
Is at hand.
Your presence is always,
Is now,
Is everywhere.
Your desire and Your demand,
Your giving is immediate.

I am already a dead man.
With You there are no excuses,
There are no conditions.
There are no alternatives.

They are
So full of excuses—
Of reasons why they can't,
Of having something else to do,
Of not being ready
Yet.
The urgency of Your heart
Is everything and everywhere, in every breath
And I am already a dead man.

And tree

You were not bearing fruit,
And your excuse was not being in season.

All my disappointment,
All my anger,
All my frustration
All my rage,
All my pain—
I turned on you,
And so you shrunk right up
And died.

Because I am a dead man,
Being in or out of season
No longer matters.
And I am already a dead man;
And only because I am already a dead man,
I can say, "yes, yes, oh yes"
To Your ever immediate desire.

KISSING

Of all of them,
I know Judas best.
He is so much like me.
Full with passion and desire.
Thirsty after righteousness.
Wounded by all the suffering.
Outraged by hypocrisy
And the perversion of You.
I know him
Well and deeply.
Of all of them,
I think I am closest to him.

And yet,
He hates me.
He is so,
So angry with me.
I will not turn
Stone into bread.
Nor will I
Force the hypocrites

To change their minds,
Their hearts.
Neither will I organize
Or plan for the future
Of our small band.
His torment
I could reach out
And touch.

His anguish wails up
From the silence
Of his eyes.
And he will have
To do something
To make it go his way.
His love
Is for the rightness, the correctness
Of godly causes.
But his love
Is not for You.
He comes so close,
And yet misses by so much.

I'm glad I chose him.
But it has taken him
Right to the eternal fires
And the gnashing of teeth.

A good and righteous
Human being
Who believes
That his vision
Of righteousness
Is the same as Your desire.

Oh, Judas,
We have kissed before,
And we will kiss again;

And I know you hate me.
Into the arms

Of the All Merciful One,
I commit you.

GENEROSITY

I have listened carefully
To the words
They use to describe me.
They are very generous
In the offering
Of their opinions
And their descriptions.
"Blasphemer!
Is familiar to my ears
And "troublemaker!" too.
Sometimes, "revolutionary,"
And sometimes, "possessed!"
But what I hear
Most often is,
"Unclean, dirty, seedy, filthy,
... defiled." It is my destruction
Of the cherished illusion
That You
Have something to do
With the cleanness and purity
That troubles them

Most.
They want their religion
Whitewashed, bleached out,
Precious,
Preciously respectable,
And they judge
What acts are clean
And pure and good,

And what acts are dirty,
And corrupt, and bad,
And they tell us
What people are clean
And pure and good
And what people
Are dirty and impure and bad,
And they warn
Not to defile
Ourselves
By touching,
Eating, sitting.
They don't want You.

With the unclean.
And with their
Idolatry of Holy cleanliness
And pure righteousness,
      they are the defilers—they are the defilers.
They,
Have defiled You.
For You are
The maker and lover
Of all.
Even of them.

And so it is
I sit with the unclean,
And eat with the impure,
And walk with the outcasts,

And talk with the dirty;
And my garment
Is not pure white.
They cannot stand
My seediness.
Of all things,
That outrages them the most.

THE DREAM AGAIN

Again,
The dream.
Now I am within the cave.
The monster is awake,
And crushed apples
And honey no longer suffice.
Now it wants me.
It needs me.
And I walk towards its mouth.
I will give myself
To this monster.
I will enter its mouth
And die on its spiked teeth.
Food, to be eaten,
To fill him and to change him.
Close now.
Very close.

FOUND WITH THE BODY AND THE JOURNAL

As I begin to write, I look down at my hands—old now, the skin mottled with prominent veins, knuckles protruding. Where once there was a graceful line from nail to hand, the line now bellies out and caves in as it maps the year's toll. I am an old woman. My hands are both witness to and evidence of the passage of years since I was taught to read and write as a little girl. Then your hands guided my fingers moving them up and down as I pointed a stick at the sand. No one would have expected me to read and write. What would be the use? But, you said I must learn it for you.

Even as a little girl I would have done anything you asked— so much did I love following you around, listening to your stories . . . and now it's time to tell your story. Pass on what your hands and life gave me and write what my eyes saw at the hard end of your life. So much to remember as I unroll the parchments you handed me that last night in Jerusalem before they came for you. You gave me your journals and told me to hide them and that I would know when it was time to bring them to the light. Oh Rabboni, after all these years there is till danger in following you. But nowadays people come. "Tell us," they say, "what you knew of Jesus of Nazareth."

I'll begin by telling what I saw as you began to move out of the world of our childhood. You explained that the deep love we shared would be the more intense for not marrying and making a family. Your life was to be dedicated to other causes and I should make a life on my own. But I couldn't let you go and spent my time following along in the crowds which began to be part of your life as soon as you started healing and teaching. When you were tired, you would come to me and sleep in a corner and I would feel a possessive pride that you came to me, not Peter, not John. Then you would leave all too quickly to go out again, making enemies as fast as you made followers. I would beg you to stop, stay and be safe hidden with me. You would explain impatiently that your time was limited and there was much to do. Each time it was painful to see you go carrying nothing, counting on God to provide yet sometimes you returned hungry.

When I followed in the crowds, I would listen to what they said: The suspicious, the hostile ones, the curious, and the political, wanting to believe that you would be the leader of a new movement which would liberate us from Roman rule. Other times when you were with me, I would prepare food, rub your shoulders, wash your dusty stained feet and pretend to myself that we were a couple. It was never long because soon there would be an interruption—someone at the door asking for help and you would go even in the middle of the night.

But if you slept, you had dreams, messages from God you

called them, and you would tell them to me and I would be scared of your darkness. I wanted simple things, human things, happy endings that would make me celebrate.

The other disciples wanted you to tell them yet another story—one of power and glory and dominion, but you gave none of us what we hoped for. The day you asked Peter to tell you who he thought you were was the first time you told us about Jerusalem and what would happen there. Suffering and loss. When you gave me your scrolls, all I knew was fear—fear about what would happen to you, fear about what would happen to us if you were gone. So, as you were led to the house of the high priest, I followed once again in the crowd, this time an angry one, as you walked calmly and silently among them. As we walked more and more people joined the crowd, curious and watchful. Outside the house we sat in the courtyard all now waiting, waiting for the word of your fate. Every so often someone would come forth from the house, but none of us dared go in. When someone came out, we would ask him to describe what was happening. They said you stood stooped with weariness while man after man testified of your teachings, your blasphemous acts in the temple. Finally, one who exited told us of your claiming your identity and I knew that your death was near.

Early the next morning, it seemed all the enemies you had made during your ministry collected outside the house swelling the crowd still further. You were bound and accompanied by armed guards as you were walked over to the governor's house where you would be sentenced. Pilate was a little man, not anxious to get into the middle of this Jewish squabble. When he heard you were from Galilee, he rejoiced inwardly and passed you on to Herod's jurisdiction. So, again you were walked looking more and more weary, blood and bruises showing on your body from the ill treatment you had already received. Herod questioned you about the healings you had done, your blasphemous teachings which the scribes and priests called out to him. You said nothing, now draped with a cloak as you were walked once more to Pilate enduring the crowd's abuse. We were scattered among the crowd, now too fearful to identify ourselves by protesting your treatment. Pilate again tried to release you as he sat in the judgment seat—offering the crowd the chance to substitute another criminal, three times the crowd screamed out "crucify Him!" You stood there looking sad and distracted staring at something in the distance none of us could see.

All of this noise and hostility was so different from the solemn night before you were taken. I found myself remembering it was one of the few times we had you to ourselves. Just as your disciples and you together in Jerusalem to celebrate the Passover. We were led to a place none of us had ever been before—a room in the house of one of your local followers. It was near the center of town, up some stairs, a small room with several benches and a table. There we set up the Passover meal—the lamb, the bitter herbs, the unleavened bread, and the wine. All the familiar bits and pieces of our religious life as Jews. Lit by the oil burning in the small clay lamps, the darkness yet surrounded us in that close room in Jerusalem.

Before we began the meal you did a strange thing. It was what servants would do in grand houses for the comfort of the guests. You took a pitcher of water, a basin, and some cloth and one by one you washed and dried our feet: the rough, callused, grimy feet which had followed you from town to town those past three years. When you had done, I in turn took the basin from you and dipped your feet in the muddy water drying them slowly as you smiled down at me—a look I will never forget.

At the table as we sat down we were quiet for once noticing your preoccupation and fatigue. You gave thanks and took the bread in your hands breaking it in half and passing it on to us to break off crumbs and eat them. At the same time you said something we had not heard you say before—that the bread was your body and we should eat it in your memory. None of us knew what that meant but we took it and ate staring at each other to see if anyone understood what you were saying.

When we had finished the meal, you poured what was left of the wine into the cup, blessed it, and handed it to John indicating he should drink from it and then pass it on. "This is my blood which I sacrifice for you. I shall not drink of it until I am with you again in my father's kingdom." Increasingly worried by what we didn't want to understand, we passed the cup around sipping so that all could drink. You began to speak. That was the last time we would be together this way before you would be betrayed to the authorities.

We started whispering among ourselves remembering what you had said earlier about Jerusalem, asking ourselves if you knew the identity of your betrayer. No name was spoken but when Judas got up saying he had to relieve himself and went down the stairs, we speculated as minutes passed and he did not return.

* * *

We walked, hundreds of people it seemed; some for curiosity, some eager for torture and blood from the place of judgment to the hill of punishment. Golgotha, the place parents warned their children about. Criminals died there, rabble went there to see them die. All of us in the crowd were burdened—those who carried the weight of their anger and hatred burdened also. Somehow they got a man to carry your cross, you were too enfeebled by your ordeal to bear its weight. People watched as well as walked—a woman reached out to wipe the sweat and blood from your face. A few threw pebbles and stones at you and the two others to be crucified that day. As the morning wore on, the sun shone down upon us and increased the thirst and discomfort of all who gathered. Your suffering unimaginable to us even though we watched them nail you and the two others to the crosses in the blazing heat. And then we waited upon the dying. People shouted and jeered—"Save yourself, reveal your power, make us believe!" And your answer was silence.

I stood next to your mother. She and I never close before, each jealous of the time the other spent with you. Now we leaned supporting one another weeping silently and praying that your death would come quickly. We heard you cry out but your words were not intelligible to us. Whether you were praying or asking for water was not clear. We watched hoping our presence would ease your pain yet knowing it could not, suffering our own helplessness and the loss of you, her son, my love.

There was a moment of blessedness when you seemed so grateful that one of the two others being crucified with you recognized you and knew who you really were.

Finally, when the soldiers grew tired of the waiting, they went to break the legs of the other two to hasten their death. Coming to you they discovered you had already died. The spectators and followers dispersed and still we waited there numb and lost with your sagging body hanging above us. Joseph of Arimathea who had sought and received permission from Pilate arrived and helped us take down the body. We wrapped you in linen and carried you to a cave tomb Joseph had originally intended for his own use. It was while we were in the middle of these preparations that the ground shook and the noise of falling buildings reminded us of your prediction of the destruction of the Temple. We had no more room for fear, all was grief in our throat and in our heart.

Then came the Sabbath and all of us who had loved you and grieved your loss kept to ourselves. All dispersed and alone, separated from each other as we were from you. The day passed as slowly as we believed all the ones to come would pass without the life that had filled our lives with meaning and connection.

Early the next morning some of the women and I set out for your tomb bringing with us the herbs and ointments we had assembled and prepared in order to anoint your body—something we had not had time to do earlier. When we reached the tomb, we found it open with the rock which had been used to seal it rolled aside. There near the wall were the line cloths which had wrapped your body, but there was no other trace of you. Instead there was a stranger standing there, a radiant man, who told us not to cry. "Jesus is not here because he has been raised from the dead," he said. We wept not believing his words and turned to go. But as we turned, we saw another man who addressed us. It was you but I did not recognize you through my tears until I heard your voice.

When I reached out to embrace you I dropped all that I carried and you told me not to touch for you were different than before and so our relationship would have to be different as well. That was hard, very hard. I wanted nothing more than to stay with you and touch you, and instead I was to be your messenger.

That was the beginning of your new way with us. Showing up unexpected, shattering us with joy, meeting us where we were and moving us on. On the road, in the way, on the mountaintop there you would be—your spirit bigger than life not judging those of us who had abandoned you in the past but empowering us for the future, changing us all in all.

Telling us of forgiveness, charging us to tell that death is not the end of life. And so it continues unto this day and I, an old woman, honored by these memories, remember still, my time is to come soon—no children—no husband but one great, great love—a love touched and nurtured by these old hands— fully filled—Selah.

ABOUT THE AUTHOR

Michael Dwinell, educator, consultant, and counselor for spiritual formation has been helping clients deepen, intensify, quicken, and expand their sacred interiority for over three decades. Michael is a graduate of Harvard University and Virginia Theological Seminary and was ordained into the Episcopal priesthood in 1968, where he served for thirty-five years. Today, as Lay Brother Michael Simon, he is a member of the Order of Christian Workers.

Michael has consulted to numerous parishes, religious organizations, and judicatories, and continues as supervisor for numerous clergy in their professional work and personal spiritual growth.

Michael is an award-winning, published, poet and author. His doctoral thesis became his first book, BEING PRIEST TO ONE ANOTHER. GODBIRTHING followed, and FROM WITHIN THE HEART OF GOD is his most recent book. He lives with his wife, Deborah, and German Shepherd, Dexter Dunbar in Saco, Maine.

For those readers who wish to make reference to the New Testament, the following narratives from the four Gospels were reflected upon from the journal of Jesus.

The Slaughter of the Innocents
The Baptism of Jesus
The Temptation of Jesus
Jesus at Dinner
The Beheading of John
Jesus at the Wedding
The Man in the Tree
Confronting the Demons
The Annunciation
Denouncing of His Mother
The Woman at the Well
The Feeding of the Five Thousand
The Woman with the Issue of Blood
The Raising of Lazarus
The Transfiguration
Walking on Water
Cleansing of the Temple
Cursing of the Fig Tree

Printed in the United States
987100003B